Top-Secret Science

capstone
classroom

BTR Zone (Bridge to Reading) is published by Capstone Classroom, 1710 Roe Crest Drive, North Mankato, Minnesota 56003
www.capstoneclassroom.com

ISBN 978-1-62521-100-2

Editorial Credits

Eric Manske, designer; Eric Gohl, media researcher

Photo Credits

AP Photo: 40, Denver Post/R. J. Sangosti, 4, Department of State, 52; DVIC: USAF/Master Sgt. Scott Reed, cover, 57, USAF/SrA Tristin English, 8, USAF/SSGT Jocelyn Ford, 24–25, USAF/SSGT Suzanne M. Day, 13, USAF/TSGT Michael Ammons, 7, USAF/TSGT Sabrina Johnson, 58–59, Royal Australian Air Force/Leading Aircraftwoman Tricia Wiles, 11; Getty Images: AFP/Paul J. Richards, 19, AFP/Yoshikazu Tsuno, 22, Time Life Pictures/Bernard Hoffman, 28, Time Life Pictures/Ed Clark, 35, Time Life Pictures/Marie Hansen, 32, UIG/Education Images, 48; iStockphotos: alengo, 16; Library of Congress: 26, 31, 37; NASA: 43, 44, 46–47; Newscom: Getty Images/AFP, 50, LNI/ZUMA Press, 15, RIA Nowosti/akg-images, 38, Robert Caplan Photography, 20–21, ZUMA Press/Gene Blevins, 54

Design Elements: Shutterstock

About the Cover

The United States uses spy drones, such as the MQ-1 Predator, to keep an eye on its enemies.

Printed in the United States of America in North Mankato, Minnesota.
032013   007223CGF13

TABLE OF CONTENTS

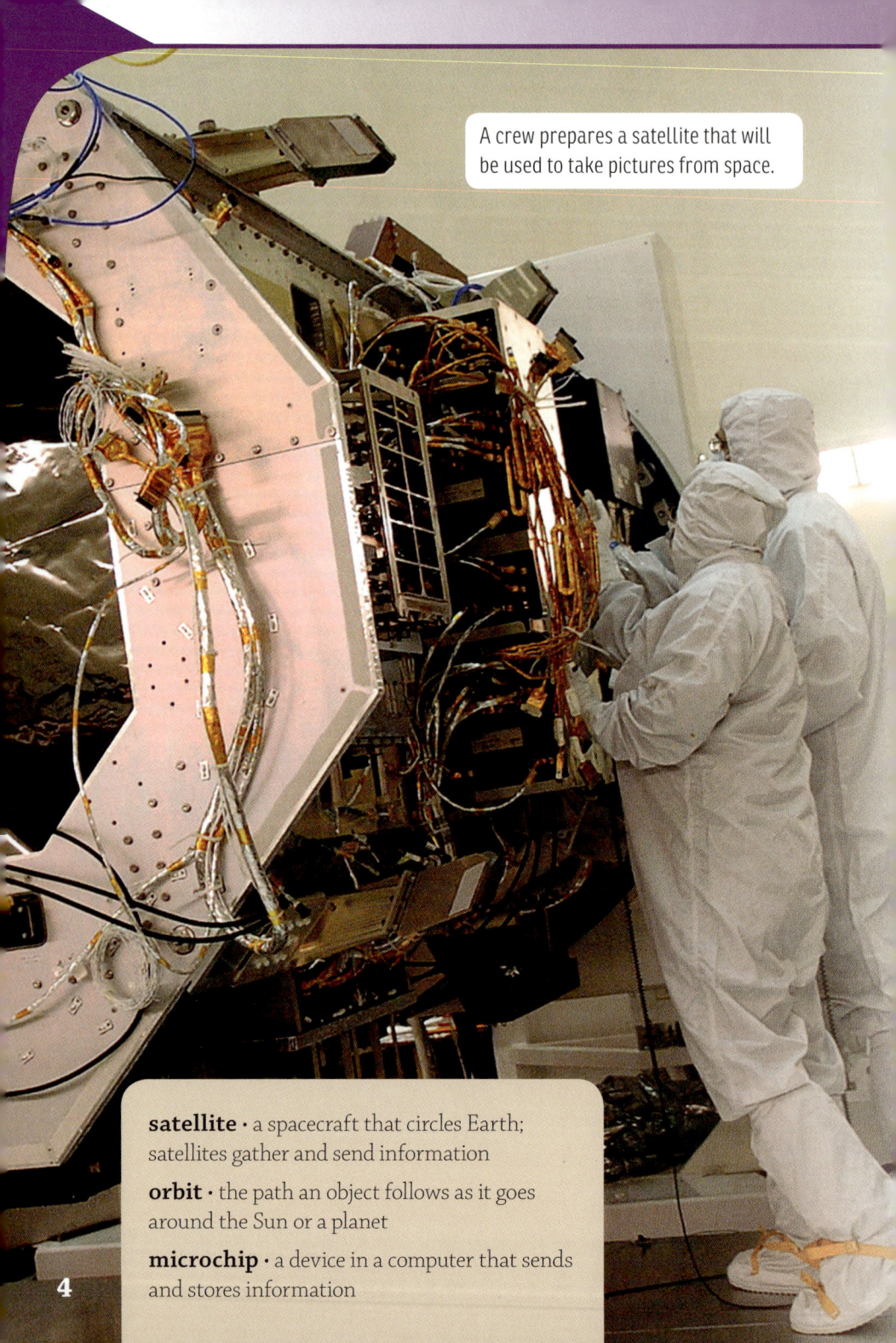

A crew prepares a satellite that will be used to take pictures from space.

satellite · a spacecraft that circles Earth; satellites gather and send information

orbit · the path an object follows as it goes around the Sun or a planet

microchip · a device in a computer that sends and stores information

CHAPTER 1

Stealth

Secrets Save Lives

The United States government is responsible for protecting the country's more than 310 million people. What is the government's biggest weapon? Technology! The government uses all kinds of high-tech equipment to keep the country safe. **Satellites** with sensitive cameras are one important technology. These machines **orbit**, or travel around, Earth. They watch our enemies from thousands of miles away. Computer **microchips** can be hidden almost anywhere. These small devices send and store information. They help our government keep us safe. Robots have been designed to help fight wars. All of these technologies save human lives.

Designing these technologies can take many years and is expensive. The U.S. government can't afford to let its research fall into the wrong hands. That's why this research is kept secret. We're not allowed to know about the newest technologies. But we can look at the top-secret technologies of the past. This book explores how secret technology has been used throughout U.S. history.

Stealth Bomber

Imagine: U.S. warplanes, like the B-2 stealth bomber, are speeding toward enemy targets. Each plane is seen as a moving dot on computer screens at the U.S. command center. The enemy is expecting an attack. They too are watching their computer screens. But their screens are blank. They cannot see the approaching enemy aircraft. Boom! The first bombs hit their targets. The enemy is surprised. Were the planes invisible? Why didn't they see them coming?

Stealth bombers are designed for secrecy.

The stealth bomber's shape and color make it difficult to see in the sky. It is also a quiet plane. Its engine is located deep inside the plane's body to muffle its noise. Stealth bombers are also designed to be invisible to sensors. Sensors are devices that receive and send signals. Though all governments monitor the air space above their countries, they can't see the stealth bomber coming toward them.

A computer screen shows planes detected by radar.

How the Stealth Avoids Detection

Radar is a system that monitors the sky for aircraft. Strong radio waves are sent into the sky. The waves are signals that bounce off large objects, like a plane, and travel back toward Earth. Radar detectors on the ground pick up the signal. The detectors use the signal to locate planes in the sky.

The stealth bomber is covered in a special material that absorbs radio waves. The plane's curved shape causes radio waves to bounce off it in unusual directions. Both of these features keep radar detectors from "seeing" the stealth.

Infrared sensors can detect heat and use it to find a plane's location. **Exhaust** from a plane is usually very hot. Before these gases from the stealth leave the plane, they pass through a cooling chamber. The exhaust is cool by the time it leaves the plane. This makes the stealth bomber invisible to infrared sensors.

radar · a device that uses radio waves to track the location of objects

infrared · light that produces heat; humans cannot see infrared light

exhaust · the waste gases produced by an engine

Smart Bombs

Throughout history, people have worked to make better weapons, especially ones that are launched or sent out into the air. Launched weapons can be arrows, bullets, bombs, and missiles. These weapons are successful only if they can hit their target. Modern technology has improved some bombs so much that they are now considered "smart." Smart bombs have sensors and computers in them. This technology allows them to be guided to their target with great accuracy.

Some smart bombs have infrared video cameras on them. These cameras detect heat. When such a bomb is launched, it shows the pilot a video of its flight. The pilot can guide the smart bomb as if it were a remote-controlled plane. The bomb can be sent directly to its target.

Because these cameras detect heat and not light, they can find their target even in the dark. Other smart bombs have **laser**-seeking sensors on them. A military team on the ground shines a narrow, powerful beam of light, or laser beam, on a target. The laser-seeking sensor on the bomb senses this and flies directly to the target.

A laser-guided bomb is loaded onto a fighter jet.

laser · a device used to send out a powerful beam of energy

Precision-Guided Bombs

More advanced smart bombs use **GPS** (global positioning systems) to guide them to their targets. GPS is a tool that uses satellites orbiting Earth to find the location of objects on the ground. Smart bombs that use GPS are programmed with the exact location of the target before they are launched. The computer on board the bomb uses GPS to check its position as it moves through the sky. The computer keeps the bomb aimed at the target by moving the bomb's tail fins. This steers the bomb through the air.

Unlike laser-guided and infrared bombs, this type of smart bomb does not need to "see" its target. It can be used in all types of weather. This is an advantage because weather can affect the other bombing methods.

GPS · stands for global positioning system; an electronic tool used to find the location of an object

Smart bombs are more expensive than regular bombs. However, there are some important reasons to use them. Smart bombs can change their course once they are in the air. That makes them very effective at hitting specific targets. The bomb's accuracy helps protect innocent people who might be near a targeted area.

A GPS-guided bomb blows up a cave in Iraq.

Lasers in the Sky

In the 1980s President Ronald Reagan supported research for developing high-powered lasers for military use. Lasers would be used to destroy enemy missiles headed toward our country or military zones. Researchers found that high-powered lasers would work best if they were aimed down at Earth from space. But the technology at the time was not advanced enough to make this a reality.

Scientists continue to research how lasers can be used as **offensive** and **defensive weapons**. Offensive weapons are used against enemies. Defensive weapons are used for protection from enemy weapons. Today there are strong lasers aboard special aircraft. These lasers are used to find and destroy missiles.

offensive weapons · military weapons used to attack an enemy

defensive weapons · military weapons used for protection against an enemy

Land-based lasers could some day provide protection against attacks from the sky.

A Secret Lab

How do scientists come up with so many amazing ideas? Area 51 is a secretive research lab in Nevada. Here scientists design new and improved aircraft. Some people believe that an alien ship crashed to Earth in this area. Some people believe scientists there are learning new technologies from the alien spacecraft.

An "electronic footprint" isn't really a footprint. It's the record kept by computers of everything a user does.

data · information or facts

CHAPTER 2

Electronically You

Electronic Footprints

Technology is a part of our everyday lives. We all know about cell phones and the Internet. We shop online and use websites called search engines to do research. We write e-mails and instant text messages. We connect with friends through electronic social media. And this technology automatically keeps a record of everything you do. This record is called your "electronic footprint." You may think that what you do online is private. It's not.

Some companies study your electronic footprint. They use **data**, or information, from the sites you visit online to see what interests you. They then use the information to try to sell specific products to you. Next time you go online from your home computer, look at the ads that appear on your screen. You will probably notice that they are for websites you have recently visited. Companies that collect this information sell it to other companies for their own advertising.

Footprints Tell Secrets

The U.S. government also looks at electronic footprints. The National Security Agency (NSA) uses machines to "watch" what Americans are doing online. The machines look for any kind of questionable activity. The NSA uses this data to identify and find anyone who may be a threat to our country.

Police officers use electronic footprints to help them solve crimes. Many cars now have a GPS unit installed under the hood. This device can tell a police officer where a person drove and how fast they were going. This information can help police understand what happened during an accident. Cell phones also have GPS. Police use it to track down suspects. Some police cars now have special cameras that scan license plates on passing cars. Police check the scans against all registered license plates. This tells the police the car owner's name and if he or she has broken any laws.

Police use a special camera to scan license plates.

Facial Recognition

Throughout history, people have recognized their friends by looking at their faces. In the past 100 years, fingerprints have been used to identify individuals. Today we use **DNA profiling** and other modern technology. DNA profiling compares samples of human material to decide if they are from the same person.

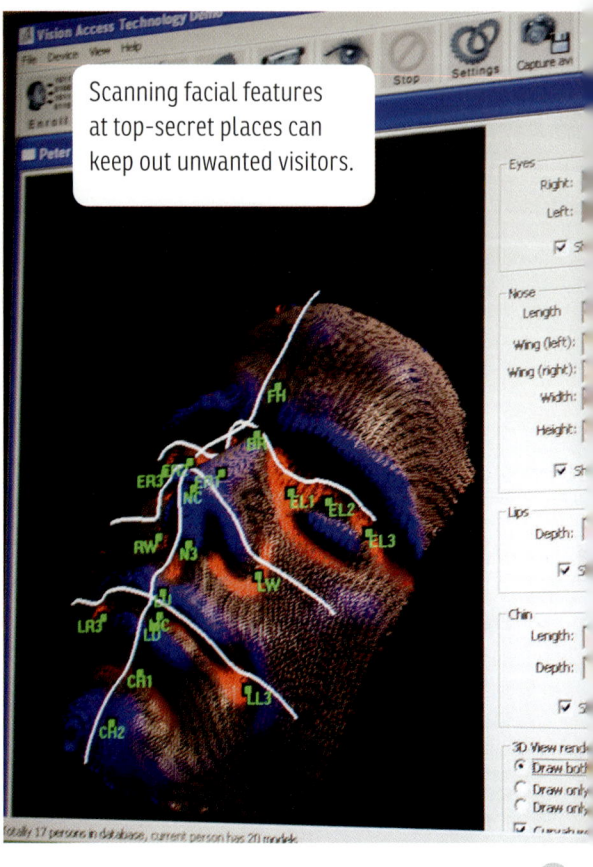

Scanning facial features at top-secret places can keep out unwanted visitors.

Certain kinds of cameras can take 3D pictures of faces. Computer software then identifies facial features by comparing them with the 3D pictures of faces in a database, or a group of computer files that holds information. By matching a real face to a 3D picture, the software can tell who someone is. These cameras can be used at security desks. They check the identity of people who pass by. The software is so accurate it can even tell the difference between identical twins.

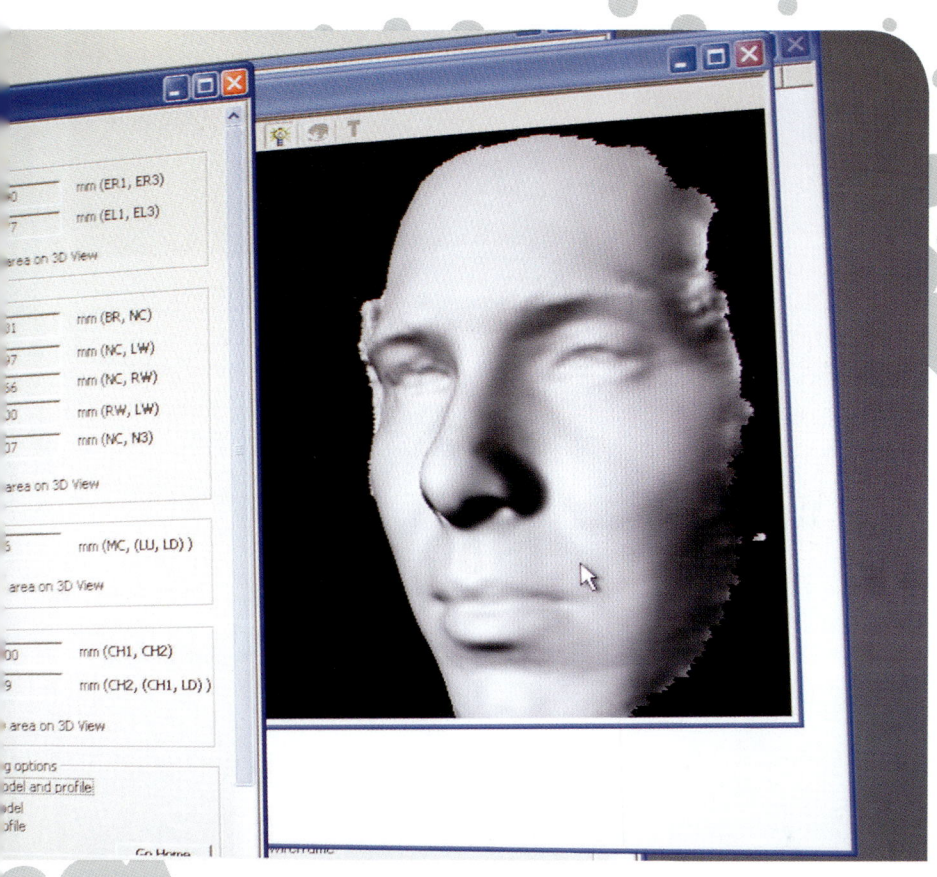

The following text is visible in the software interface in the image:

mm (ER1, ER3)
mm (EL1, EL3)
area on 3D View

mm (BR, NC)
mm (NC, LW)
mm (NC, RW)
mm (RW, LW)
mm (NC, N3)
area on 3D View

mm (MC, (LU, LD))
area on 3D View

mm (CH1, CH2)
mm (CH2, (CH1, LD))
area on 3D View

g options
odel and profile
del
file

Go Home

Technology in Your Pocket

Some smartphones work like 3D cameras. These cameras can be used to create a 3D **avatar**, or computer image, that looks a lot like the real person. These cameras are used more for fun than security, but the technology is the same.

DNA profiling · the process of comparing DNA samples to determine if they are from the same person; DNA stands for deoxyribonucleic acid

avatar · a digital image that represents a person

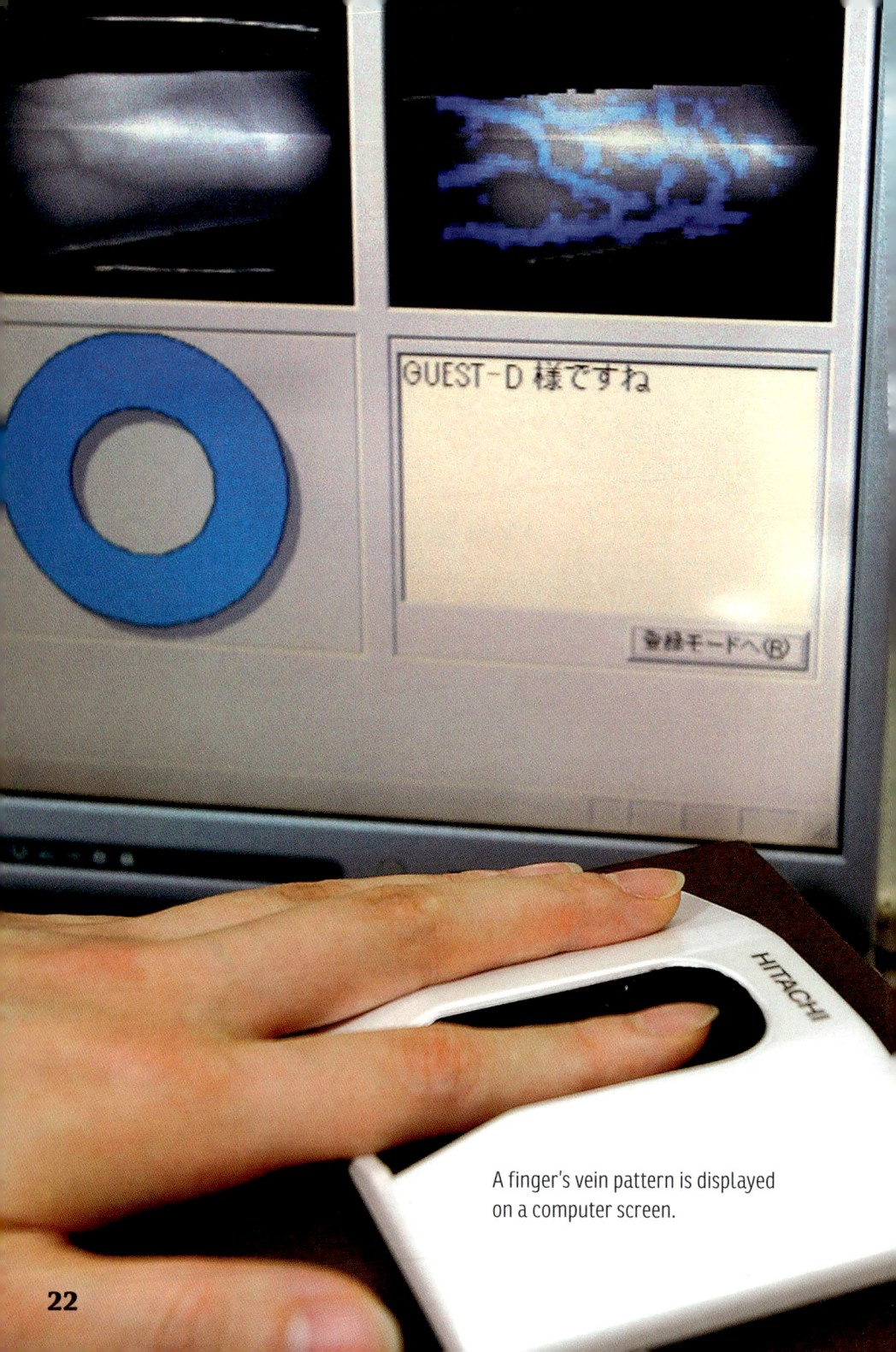

GUEST−D 様ですね

登録モードへ(R)

HITACHI

A finger's vein pattern is displayed
on a computer screen.

Vein Patterns

Some public and private places need to be extremely secure because they contain secret information. No one can enter these areas without permission. In such situations, biometrics can be very useful. **Biometrics** is the science of using physical features to identify a person.

Take a look at the **veins** that are visible on the back of your hands. This pattern of blood vessels is unique. Plastic surgery can change someone's face. There are ways to create a false fingerprint. Unlike those physical features, vein patterns cannot be changed or faked.

Vein patterns can be used as a method of biometric identification. A special infrared camera works like an **X-ray**, except it takes a picture of veins, not bones. The picture taken is compared to the vein patterns of everyone who is allowed past a certain point. If your pattern doesn't match, you can't go in!

biometrics · a system where a person's unique physical qualities are used to identify them

vein · a blood vessel that carries blood back to the heart

X-ray · a picture taken of the inside of the body

Eye Recognition

Another physical feature that cannot be changed is the **iris**. The iris is the part of the eye that has color, such as brown or blue. It circles the dark center of the eye called the **pupil**. Scientists have created iris scanners to identify people. An iris scanner is a small device that is attached to a wall. A person stands a few inches away from it and looks directly at the scanner. The scanner uses two types of light to take a detailed picture of the eye. It takes a picture of the pupil, iris, eyelid, and eyelashes. It then analyzes the size and shape of these features.

iris · the round colored part of your eye

pupil · the round, dark center of your eye

Voice Recognition

Computers in our homes, cars, and phones can recognize our voices. This type of recognition software is not used for security reasons. It is used to help us in our daily lives. This technology allows us to control machines without having to use our hands. A person can turn on lights in their home with the sound of their voice rather than with a flip of a switch.

The U.S. military uses eye recognition technology.

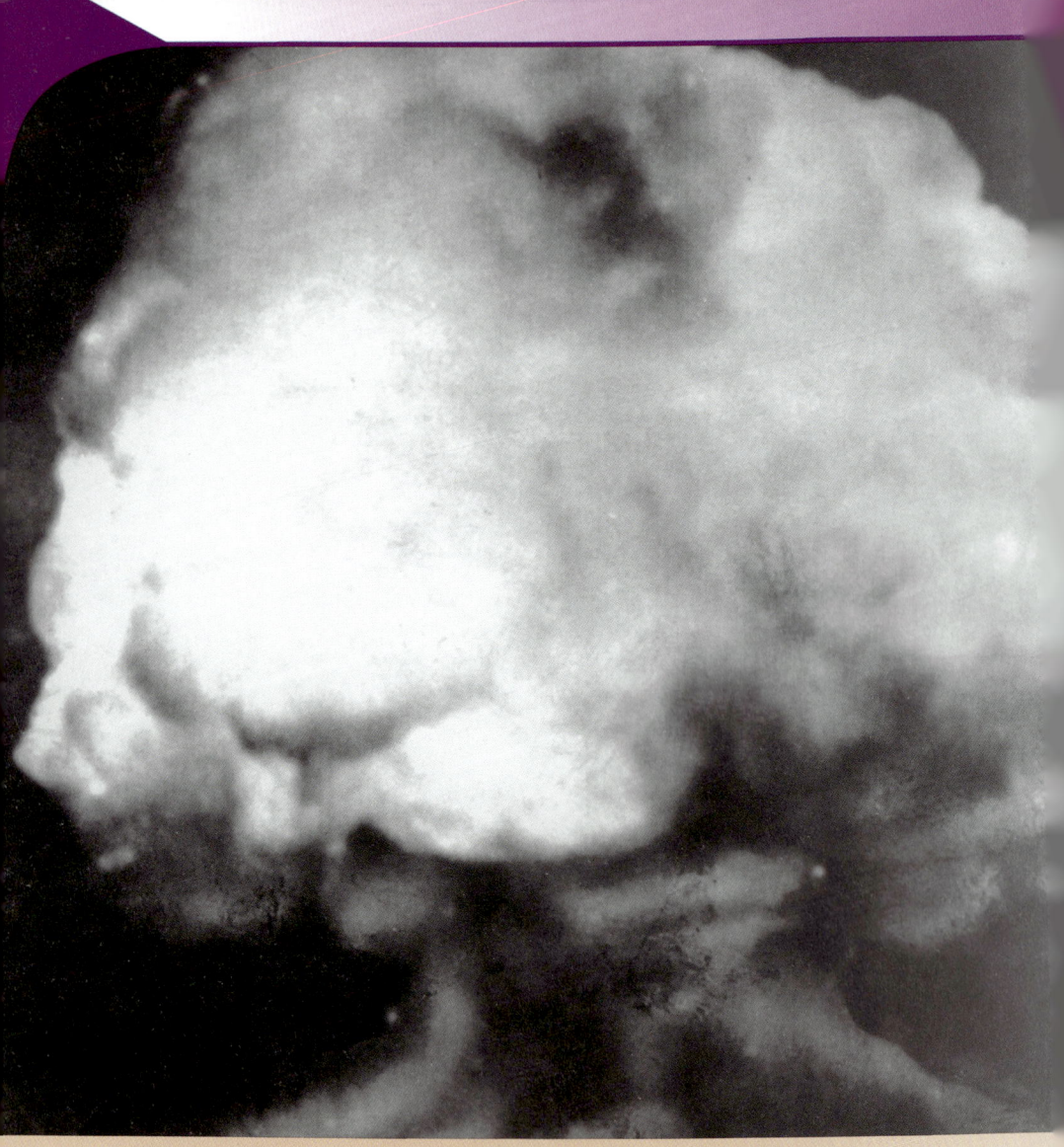

A mushroom-shaped cloud filled the sky in New Mexico on July 16, 1945.

bunker · a strongly built room or building set beneath the ground to offer protection

crater · a large hole made by an object smashing into the ground

atomic bomb · a powerful explosive that destroys large areas

CHAPTER 3

Manhattan Project

The Atomic Bomb

Before dawn on July 16, 1945, a group of scientists and government officials huddled together in an underground room, or **bunker**. They were working on one of the most top-secret projects in U.S. history, the Manhattan Project.

They stared out at the empty New Mexico desert. As the seconds ticked by, tension grew. No one was really sure what was about to happen. Suddenly, there was a tremendous explosion and a blinding flash lit up 200 miles (322 kilometers) of the desert. The explosion blasted a huge **crater** (hole) in the earth. It blew out windows 100 miles (161 km) away. A cloud 40,000 feet (12,192 meters) tall filled the sky. The scientists had just witnessed the first test of an **atomic bomb**. It was a success, but the mood in the bunker was a mixture of joy and worry. Had they just created a weapon that could wipe out the human race?

Splitting the Atom

An atom is the smallest part of an **element**.
An element is a basic building block of matter. Every
atom has a tightly packed center called the **nucleus**.
An atomic explosion occurs when the nuclei or
center of atoms are split. This process is called **fission**.
When the nuclei are split, a large amount of energy
is released.

Scientists worked on
an atom smasher used
for atomic fission in 1941.

The **periodic table** is a list of elements. Each element is made of different atoms. Different types of atoms release different amounts of energy during fission. Uranium is an element that releases a large amount of energy during fission. Uranium is used in atomic bombs.

element · a substance made of atoms that cannot be broken down into simpler substances

nucleus · the center of an atom

fission · the splitting apart of the nucleus of an atom to create large amounts of energy

periodic table · the chart of the chemical elements arranged according to their atomic numbers

World War: Axis and Allies

In the 1930s **physicists** around the world were experimenting with fission reactions. These experiments helped them learn more about the energy stored in atoms. It wasn't until World War II (1939–1945) that fission was used to make bombs.

In the early 1940s, Germany, Japan, Italy, and other countries formed an **alliance**. This group of nations was called the Axis. Fighting the Axis were the Allies. The United States, Canada, the United Kingdom, Australia, the Soviet Union, China, and others made up the Allies.

The governments of the Axis countries required physicists to use their knowledge of fission to develop powerful bombs.

physicist · a scientist who studies matter and energy

alliance · an agreement between nations or groups of people to work together

British Prime Minister Winston Churchill, U.S. President Franklin D. Roosevelt, and Soviet Union Premier Joseph Stalin were leaders of the Allies.

Work on the bombs was done in extreme secrecy. The Axis countries wanted to keep this technology from reaching the hands of the Allies. Having the most powerful weapon would be a sure way to win the war.

The Manhattan Project

Physicists Albert Einstein and Enrico Fermi left their homes in Europe for the United States. Once in the United States, they learned from European scientists that German researchers were using fission to build bombs. Fearing what the Axis would do with such powerful bombs, they wrote a letter to President Franklin Delano Roosevelt. They urged him to start an atomic research program in the United States. In 1941 this program began. Its code name was the "Manhattan Project."

Leslie Groves (left) and Robert Oppenheimer (right) oversaw work on the Manhattan Project.

The Manhattan Project was top secret. Only a small group of Allied scientists and officials knew about it. Robert Oppenheimer was the leader of the scientists. Leslie Groves, a general in the Army Corps of Engineers, was the project's overall leader. These men and their staff contributed greatly to the development of the first atomic bomb. They worked at a research facility in Los Alamos, New Mexico. Secrecy was so important that even the bomb had a code name: "Gadget." Oppenheimer and Groves were in the bunker when Gadget exploded.

Oak Ridge, Tennessee

Even though only a small group of people knew about the Manhattan Project, 120,000 people contributed to it. Many of these people lived in the top-secret town of Oak Ridge, Tennessee. In the early 1940s, the U.S. government designed and built this town. It was a secret place for regular people to live and work. There were grocery stores, churches, and baseball fields. Oak Ridge looked like a typical small town except for the large security fence around it. Guards patrolled the fence to keep unwanted people out. What was going on in this town?

The people of Oak Ridge worked in plants and factories that **enriched** (improved) uranium. Once the uranium was enriched, it was sent to the atomic research center in Los Alamos, New Mexico. There, it was used to build atomic weapons. Even though Oak Ridge's townspeople knew they worked with uranium, they had no idea what it would be used for. The government didn't want anyone finding out. That's why they kept the whole town top secret.

enrich · to improve

A sign warns workers at a plant in Oak Ridge, Tennessee, to keep quiet.

Spies Everywhere

During the 1940s spies and secrets were everywhere. The Manhattan Project was so secretive that different groups working for it didn't know what each other did. Countries spied on other countries, even if they were on the same side!

One spy managed to sneak the secrets of the Manhattan Project out of the country. Klaus Fuchs was one of the scientists building bombs for the Allies. Throughout the 1940s he secretly gave information to the Soviet Union. The United States didn't realize what he had done until 1949, when the Soviets **detonated**, or exploded, their first atomic bomb. This action set the United States and the Soviet Union in a fierce competition to be the leading atomic power.

detonate · to cause something to explode

The End of the War

In August 1945 the United States dropped atomic bombs on the Japanese cities of Hiroshima and Nagasaki. These bombs killed thousands of people and led to the end of World War II. A peace agreement was soon signed by most of the countries involved.

A Japanese citizen photographed the bombing of Nagasaki.

The First Person in Space

In 1961 the Soviet Union's Yuri Gagarin became the first person in space. He orbited Earth in a tiny spacecraft. Less than a month later, astronaut Alan Shepard became the first American in space.

CHAPTER 4

Space Race

Sputnik

During the 1950s the Americans and Soviets competed to be the first nation to reach outer space. They were not willing to share new technology. The space programs of both countries were heavily guarded secrets.

In 1957 the Soviets caught Americans by surprise. They had launched the first satellite into space. *Sputnik I* was a small satellite that orbited Earth. It was a breakthrough that grabbed the attention of the world. Americans saw it as a threatening eye in the sky. It made them feel unsafe. The United States had missed its opportunity to be the first nation in space. This fact made the U.S. government determined to make the next big breakthrough.

Sputnik I launched the Soviet Union and the United States into a "space race."

Cold War

The United States and the Soviet Union were allies during World War II. However, the governments never fully trusted each other due to their differences. The United States was a **capitalist** country. Under capitalism, individuals own property. The Soviet Union was **communist.** Under communism, the government owns all the property. After Klaus Fuchs gave away the secret of the atomic bomb, the United States grew even more distrustful of the Soviets.

The Soviet Union showed off long-range missiles during a military parade in 1967.

Rocket Research

Wernher von Braun was part of a team of German scientists that developed rockets during World War II. In 1945 his team was captured by the Allies. The scientists were sent to Texas to do rocket research for the U.S. Army.

Tension built between both countries. They competed to build bigger and better weapons. The space race was part of this international competition. From 1945 to 1991, the two countries were part of many conflicts throughout the world. This period of time is known as the Cold War. It was a "cold" war because neither side fired weapons at the other.

capitalist · having to do with supporting capitalism; capitalism is a way of organizing a country so that property is owned by individuals

communist · having to do with supporting communism; communism is a way of organizing a country so that all the land, houses, and factories belong to the government or community

41

President Kennedy's Message

In 1961 the Soviets reached outer space before the Americans did. That same year they secretly delivered powerful missiles to Cuba. Cuba is a communist country located just south of Florida. Many Americans became very nervous when they learned Soviet missiles were so close.

President John F. Kennedy managed to get the Soviets to remove the missiles from Cuba. It wasn't enough. He felt a great pressure to beat the Soviets at something important. In May 1961 he announced that an American would be the first person to walk on the moon. It was a daring promise. Could they do it?

Kennedy worked closely with the National Aeronautics and Space Administration (NASA) to plan the *Apollo 11* mission. The mission was accomplished on July 20, 1969. That was the day American astronaut Neil Armstrong became the first person to walk on the moon.

"I believe that this nation should commit itself to achieving the goal, before this decade is out, of landing a man on the Moon and returning him safely to the Earth."

—President John F. Kennedy, May 25, 1961